JOHN HOLT
PRINTER AND POSTMASTER

SOME FACTS AND DOCUMENTS RELATING
TO HIS CAREER

By VICTOR HUGO PALTSITS
CHIEF OF THE AMERICAN HISTORY DIVISION
AND KEEPER OF MANUSCRIPTS

NEW YORK
PUBLIC LIBRARY
1920

Z
232
.H76
P2

REPRINTED, OCTOBER 1920
FROM THE
BULLETIN OF THE NEW YORK PUBLIC LIBRARY
OF SEPTEMBER, 1920

PRINTED AT THE NEW YORK PUBLIC LIBRARY
form p-145 [x-13-20 4c]

In the interest of creating a more extensive selection of rare historical book reprints, we have chosen to reproduce this title even though it may possibly have occasional imperfections such as missing and blurred pages, missing text, poor pictures, markings, dark backgrounds and other reproduction issues beyond our control. Because this work is culturally important, we have made it available as a part of our commitment to protecting, preserving and promoting the world's literature. Thank you for your understanding.

JOHN HOLT—PRINTER AND POSTMASTER
SOME FACTS AND DOCUMENTS RELATING TO HIS CAREER

By Victor Hugo Paltsits
Chief of the American History Division and Keeper of Manuscripts

JOHN HOLT, born in 1721, was a native of Williamsburg, Virginia. He received a good education and became a merchant, rising also to be Mayor of Williamsburg. But he met with financial reverses and in 1754, through family influence, secured the appointment as one of the two deputy postmasters-general for America, being stationed at New Haven, Conn. It is probable that Holt learned the printing business at Williamsburg from his brother-in-law, William Hunter, the well-established public printer.[1] About 1775, Holt set up a printing business at Norfolk, Virginia, which was superintended by his son, John Hunter Holt, of which more anon. This firm published *The Virginia Gazette, or the Norfolk Intelligencer*, under the firm's name of John H. Holt and Company.

In 1754, James Parker, printer of New York City and Woodbridge, New Jersey, was appointed postmaster of New Haven, Connecticut, and John Holt was his deputy. Here Parker established a newspaper, the *Connecticut Gazette*, which was the first newspaper printed in that colony. The printing press had been set up by Benjamin Franklin on invitation of President Clap of Yale College, with the intention of having Benjamin Mecom conduct it, but Mecom declined at the time, so Franklin sold the materials to James Parker, who began the *Connecticut Gazette* on April 12, 1755. On December 13th of that year, the newspaper appeared with the copartnership name of James Parker and Co., and John Holt, as editor and junior partner, conducted the printing business of the firm in New Haven, as well as the post-office, whilst Parker was busied with his printing-house in New York City. In the summer of 1760, Holt removed to New York. Parker's *New-York Gazette and Weekly Post-Boy*, on July 31, 1760, appeared with the imprint of James Parker and Company, Holt being again the junior partner. They also controlled the postriders from New York to Hartford, who met the postriders from Boston.[2] This partnership was dissolved on May 6, 1762, when Holt became the sole publisher, he having hired the business from Parker. He continued to announce the fact in his newspaper's colophon for several years, as, for example, in no. 1125, July 26, 1764, where the colophon reads: "New-York, Broad-Street, near the Exchange: Printed by John Holt, late Partner in this Paper, and the

---
[1] Hildeburn. *Printers and Printing in Colonial New York*, 89–98.
[2] *Post-Boy*, Apr. 8, 1762.

[3]

Printing Business in New-York, with James Parker, who has resign'd that Business in this City to him." In this issue Holt gives a good look into the postal hazards of newspaper subscribers, which is interesting and bears relationship to other judgments pronounced by him on the conduct of the post office, therefore is reproduced here, viz.:

"*Conclusion of the Reflections begun in our last, concerning the new Regulations in the Post Office.*

"In the Business of News-Papers sent by the Post, this new Act will occasion great Revolutions, if not wholly put a Stop to it, unless the Gentlemen concern'd, and all who desire the Continuance of a Business so entertaining and useful to the Publick, will contribute their Aid in their several Stations, to its Encouragement: Those who have Papers sent them, by making punctual Payments; — The Riders, by faithfully delivering the Papers on the Road, at the Places, and to the Persons directed; the Persons, in whose Care they are left on the Road, in delivering them to the right Owners, and preventing others from meddling with them; and all honest Men in general, in exposing the Infamy of those who embezzle or open Papers that don't belong to them. --- These Men, who are really Thieves to the Owners of the Papers, are worse to the Printers, by robbing them of what is vastly more than the Value of the Thing stolen. — That is, the future Custom of great Numbers, who stop their Papers merely because of their frequent Disappointments in geting them. If this infamous Practice is continued, the sending News Papers by the Post must cease. — For whereas the enclosing Papers in seal'd Covers was some Security, as only here and there a harden'd, shameless Pilferer would presume to open seal'd Papers that did not belong to them, and it was seldom done, even by such, but by Stealth, — and notwithstanding this Security, the Owners so often were robbed of their Papers, that great Numbers stop'd from the Discouragement. — Now therefore that that Security is taken away, and the Papers may be read without breaking the Covers, it is not likely that many of them will get to the Hands of their Owners, and consequently most People will stop, and the Business cease, *unless it is prevented by the extraordinary Care of the Persons thro' whose Hands the Papers pass.* This, therefore, all Gentlemen who wish the Continuance of Papers by the Post, are desired particularly to attend to, otherwise they must not long expect to receive them, nor the Printers to send them.

"Another Thing necessary to be observed is, that no Letters be sent by the Post to the Printers, relating to News Papers or Advertisements, unless the Postage be paid by the Sender; for the Profits on that Business are already so small, that it will not bear any additional Burden. The Printer of this Paper in particular desires, that none of his Customers will send him any

Letters by the Post, relating to News Papers or Advertisements, without first paying the Postage. And if after this publick Notice any such unpaid Letters are sent him, the Persons who send them are desired to take Notice, that the Postage will be charged in their Accounts, or otherwise demanded of them: Also, those Persons whose Accounts are of above 12 Months standing unpaid, must expect to have the Charge of Postage to pay on the Letters that will be sent them to demand the Money."

In April, 1763, Holt announced his removal from Burling's Slip, as follows:

"The Printing Office now kept at Burling's Slip, where the Thursday's New-York Gazette is printed, will on the first of May next, Be Removed To the House where Mrs. Steel now keeps The King's Arms Tavern, near the Exchange,"[3] and in the *Laws* of the City of New York, printed by him in 1763, he called his shop "the New Printing Office, at the lower End of Broad Street, opposite the Exchange," the present Broad and Water Streets. On April 1, 1766, the "House and Lot of Ground facing the Long-Bridge," where Holt lived, was sold at public auction,[4] and from a notice in the *Post-Boy* of May 22d, we learn that Holt was "labouring under a severe Fit of Sickness, which has confined him for several Weeks past, and rendered him incapable of Business." Notwithstanding, only a week later, on Thursday, May 29, 1766, Holt issued a newspaper which he called *The New-York Journal, or General Advertiser*, no. 1, and printed in it the very interesting advertisement which follows, in explanation of the change. Parker had already published a notice in the *New York Gazette or Weekly Post Boy* on May 22d, in which he informed that "The New Printing-Office, Formerly kept in Beaver Street in this City, Is opened there again, by the Original Proprietor." Parker's advertisement appeared again in Holt's new titled paper, the *Journal*, on May 29th. Holt's advertisement reads: "THE Printer of this Paper, having from the Middle of July 1760, near 6 Years last past, (the 2 first, in Company; and the 4 last on his own Account) publish'd in this City, a Weekly News Paper, under the Title of *The New-York Gazette or Weekly Post-Boy*; And having lately deliver'd back, all the Printing Materials he had in his Hands belonging to Mr. James Parker, of whom they had been hired; and hearing that he intends to publish a News Paper in this City, when perhaps he may choose to resume the *Title* under which he formerly publish'd: The Printer hereof, desirous to prevent the Occasion of a Complaint that might possibly have been made, *That he took Advantage of a Title, which originally belong'd to, and was brought into Credit by another,* has voluntarily concluded, for the Future to publish his Paper under another Title, *The New-York Journal, or*

---
[3] *Post-Boy*, Apr., 21, 1763, no. 1059.
[4] *Post-Boy*, Feb. 27, 1766, no. 1208.

General Advertiser, and unasked, to give up (He hopes in as much Credit as he received it) the Old Title of the Paper, to Mr. Parker. A suitable Cut for the Head of the Paper, under this new Title, will be provided, as soon as convenient; and as the Printer is now completely furnish'd with Printing Materials of all Sorts, all entirely new, he proposes to carry on the Business, in a more extensive Manner than he has yet done; and hopes the Favour he has acquired as publisher of the New-York Gazette, will not be lost under the Title of *The New-York Journal, or General Advertiser,* which will be publish'd upon the same Principles, and with the same Spirit. As all his Readers can bear Witness, *That he has never shrunk from his Duty In the worst of Times,* nor deserted the Cause of Liberty and his Country, when it was most dangerous to assert them; he hopes that now, when Peace and Tranquillity, to which he has contributed to the utmost of his Abilities, are happily restored, his former Services will not be forgotten nor undistinguish'd by the favourable Notice of the Publick. When a Cause is become popular, and out of reach of Danger, Crowds are ready to offer themselves in its Favour; but it is only in Times of Difficulty and Danger, its real Friends can be certainly known. The same Writers that have given Value to the *Gazette,* will Contribute their kind Assistance to the *New-York Journal;* and as they have in dangerous Times, exerted themselves in Support of our just Rights, will be no less assiduous, now that Tranquility is restored in cultivating the Arts of Peace, and promoting the Prosperity and Happiness, both of Great Britain and her Colonies in America, who now evidently appear to be really, and truly but one People, whose Interests are united, and inseparably connected. The People of G. Britain and Ireland, the Ministry, the Parliament, King, Lords and Commons, have all approved our Cause, have stood forth in Defence of our Rights, and repeal'd the oppressive Acts, ---which appear to have been passed by Means of Surprise and Misrepresentation, and therefore ought to be ascribed wholly to a Faction, not to the People or Legislature of Great-Britain, who have deliver'd us from Oppression, and preserved us from Slavery a Ruin; and are therefore justly entitled to our most sincere and hearty Th ks, Gratitude and Love. Henceforth, may no partial Designs take Place! M the Prosperity of the *whole* British Empire, be the Object of every one's pu it, equally with his own private Advantage: And may each Individual disdain to form, or be concern'd in any Scheme for private Emolument, that is in any Respect inconsistent with Justice and the publick Good."

When Holt learned that Parker would not at the time begin a newspaper in New York, he resumed the old *Gazette* title, on June 5, 1766, as no. 1222, continuing it in that form until no. 1240 of October 9, 1766. Then on October 16th, with no. 1241, he again changed the title to *The New-York Journal, or General Advertiser,* whilst Parker, likewise on October 16th and also as no. 1241, resumed the publication of his *Gazette.* Holt's *Journal* was discontinued in New York City with the issue of August 29, 1776, no. 1756, because of the occupation of the city by the British troops early in September. Holt resumed the *Journal,* without change of numeration, on July 7, 1777, no. 1757, at Kingston, Ulster County, New York. The last issue was no. 1771, which was in October, a few days before the British invaded and burned the town. Concerning the loss of his press and effects, we have his very important letter to the New York Assembly, on February 13, 1778 (printed *infra*); also the testimony of his fellow printer, Samuel Loudon, of Fishkill, in a letter to Isaac Beers, of New Haven, on November 3, 1777,[5] in which Loudon adverts to the scarcity of paper, his own desperate need of it, and the fact that Holt "can't work for some time having lost his Press in Kingston, tho' he got his Types saved." Curiously enough, in the inventory of his estate, in 1785 (printed *infra*), there is an item for "Iron of a Press (burnt at Esopus)," which is Kingston. On May 11, 1778, Holt's paper was revived at Poughkeepsie.[6] It was continued until suspended on November 6, 1780; resumed on July 30, 1781; suspended again on January 6, 1782, while he printed the New York Laws, and resumed finally in New York City at the close of the war, on November 22, 1783, with a new series of numbers and entitled, *The Independent New York Gazette.*

Holt died in New York City, on January 30, 1784, and his body was interred in St. Paul's churchyard.[7] Isaiah Thomas, the Father of American Printing, summed up his character thus: "Holt was a man of ardent feelings, and a high churchman, but a firm whig, a good writer, and a warm advocate of the cause of his country."[8]

Reference has already been made to Holt's printing-office at Norfolk, Virginia, conducted by his son. In an issue of *The Virginia Gazette, or the Norfolk Intelligencer,* just before Dunmore ordered the seizure of the press, Holt and Company had printed some reflections on the ancestors of Dunmore, which must have angered the governor (see *Pennsylvania Gazette,* no. 2445, November 1, 1775, pp. 1 and 4). This seizure of the printing outfit caused one correspondent to protest to Dunmore that he must have known that by the law "the persons of the men, and property of the printer, were sacred." And he added: "How then could you dare invade the privileges of the one, or the property of the other, and thereby deprive the public of a press, by which their wrongs are made known, and through which all knowledge is conveyed. Must *Genius* bow the neck, and court the smiles of NERO, while *fair Science* fits melancholy, deploring her unhappy state!" The following items refer to the fate of the press and printer during Dunmore's war.[9]

---

[5] Original in New York Historical Society, Miscell. MSS.
[6] Brigham's Bibliography of American Newspapers, in *Proceedings* of American Antiquarian Society, October, 1913; April and October, 1917.
[7] Hildeburn, 96.
[8] *History of Printing in America,* I: 303.
[9] John Murray, fourth earl of Dunmore, b. 1732; d. 1809. In 1770, he was appointed governor of New York and two years later was transferred to Virginia. He was forced to flee early in 1775 and in 1776 fired Norfolk. He was defeated by Gen. Andrew Lewis, who, in the last intercolonial war, was a major under George Washington, in 1757.

"WILLIAMSBURG, October 7 [1775].

The following extract of a letter from Norfolk will serve to shew the distressed situation that town is unhappily reduced to by the wanton, unjust, and cruel behaviour of the tools of tyranny and oppression on board the ships of war in that harbour. Various reports have been in circulation here, within a few days past, of a manœuvre of the soldiery on the 30th ult. and from the communication by water being obstructed, it is seldom we get intelligence from thence: but we are assured the letter contains an authentic account.

"Extract of a letter from Norfolk, October 1.

'Yesterday came on shore about 15 of the King's soldiers, and marched up to the printing-office, out of which they took all the types and part of the press, and carried them on board the new ship *Eilbeck,* in presence, I suppose, of between two and three hundred spectators, without meeting with the least molestation; and upon the drums beating up and down the town, there were only about 35 men to arms. They say they want to print a few papers themselves; and they looked upon the press not to be free, and had a mind to publish something in vindication of their own characters. But as they have only part of the press, and no ink as yet, it is out of their power to do any thing in the printing business. They have got neither of the compositors, but I understand there is a printer on board the *Otter.* Mr. Cumming, the bookbinder, was pressed on board, but is admitted ashore at times; He says Captain Squire was very angry they did not get Mr. Holt, who happened to be in the house the whole time they were searching, but luckily made his escape, notwithstanding the office was guarded all round. Mr. Cumming also informs, that the Captain says he will return every thing in safe order to the office, after he answers his ends, which, he says, will be in about three weeks. — It was extremely melancholy to hear the cries of the women and children in the streets; most of the families are moving out of town, with the greatest expedition; the carts have been going all this day.' "[10]

"WILLIAMSBURG, October 13 [1775].

The following address was presented to Lord Dunmore, by the Corporation of Norfolk, in consequence of Mr. Holt, Printer of that borough, being robbed of his printing materials, and his servants carried off, by order of his Lordship.

'*To his Excellency the right Hon.* JOHN *Earl of* DUNMORE, *his Majesty's Lieutenant and Governor General of the colony and dominion of* Virginia, &c. &c. WE his Majesty's faithful subjects, the Mayor, Aldermen, and Common Council of the borough of Norfolk, in Common-Hall assembled, beg leave to represent to your Lordship, that on this day a party of men under the command of Captain Squire, of the Otter sloop of war, lying in this

---

[10] *Penn. Gazette,* October 18, 1775, no. 2443, p. 3.

harbour, landed in the most public part of this borough, in the most daring manner, and, in open violation of the peace and good order, seized on the printing utensils belonging to an inhabitant of this town, as well as the persons of two of his family.

'We beg leave also to represent to your Lordship that this act is both illegal and riotous; and that, together with a musket ball fired into the town yesterday, from on board the Kingfisher, has greatly alarmed and incensed the inhabitants, and has occasioned a great number of the women and children to abandon this borough; and that, if these arbitrary proceedings pass unnoticed by your Lordship, as chief magistrate of this colony, that none of the inhabitants are safe from insult and abuse. We therefore, as our duty, represent this matter to your Lordship for your interposition.

'We, my Lord, as men, and as a Common-Hall, have ever preserved the peace of this town, and have never prevented the ships of war and others from being supplied with provisions, or any other necessaries, and have carefully avoided offering any insult to any of his Majesty's servants. We had therefore hoped, that the inhabitants would never have been molested in their lawful business. We are sorry, however, to have it in our power to state this fact to your Lordship; which we must and do think a gross violation of all that men and freemen can hold dear.

'Allow us to observe to your Lordship, that if the inhabitants had been disposed to repel insult, that they were sufficiently able either to have cut off, or taken prisoners, the small party that came on shore; and this, we hope, is another proof of their peaceable intentions.

'We the Mayor, Aldermen and Common Council of the borough of Norfolk, do most earnestly entreat your Lordship that the Captains of the men of war may not reduce the inhabitants to the dreadful alternative of defending their persons, or tamely suffering themselves to be abused, and request that your Lordship will interpose your authority to put a final stop to such violent infringements of our rights, and to order the persons seized on by Captain Squire to be immediately put on shore, and the property to be replaced from whence it was taken.

'*To the Mayor, Aldermen, and Common Council, of the borough of Norfolk.*

'GENTLEMEN,

'I was an eye-witness to a party, belonging to the Otter sloop of war, landing at the hour and place you mention, and did see them bring off two of the servants belonging to the printer, together with his printing utensils; and I do really think they could not have rendered the borough of Norfolk, or the country adjacent to it, a more essential service, than by depriving them of the means of poisoning the minds of the people, and exciting in them the spirit of rebellion and sedition, and by that means drawing inevitable ruin and destruction on themselves and country. As to the illegality of the act, I am afraid some of you, in this very common hall assembled, ought to blush when you make use of the expression; as I know you cannot but be conscious that you have, by every means in your power, totally subverted the laws and constitution, and have been the advisers and abettors in throwing off all allegiance to that Majesty's crown and government, to whom you profess yourselves faithful subjects. As to the musket ball being fired into the town, I do believe there is not a man in it that is not satisfied it was an accident; and such a one as, I hope, will not happen again. But with regard to your having ever preserved the peace in your town, there is a recent proof of the contrary. As to your not repelling the insult, as you call it, or taking prisoners the small party that was on shore, I impute it to some other reasons (from your drums beating to arms during greatest part of the time that the party was on shore) than to your peaceable intentions. As to your last requisition, I do assure you that every means in my power shall be employed, both with the navy and army, to preserve the peace, good order, and happiness of the inhabitants of the borough of Norfolk, so long as they behave themselves as faithful subjects to his Majesty. I expect at the same time, that if any individual shall behave himself as your printer has done, by aspersing the characters of his Majesty's servants, and others, in the most scurrilous, false, and scandelous manner, and by being the instigator of treason and rebellion against his Majesty's crown and government, and you not take such steps as the law directs to restrain such offenders, I do then expect you will not be surprised if the military power interposes to prevent the total dissolution of all decency, order and good government. But I promise the printer, on my honour, if he will put himself and servants under my protection, that they shall not meet with the least insult, and shall be permitted to print every occurrence that happens during these unhappy disputes between the Mother Country and her Colonies, he only confining himself to truth, and representing matters in a fair, candid, impartial manner on both sides.

'This, I hope, will convince you that I had nothing more in view, when I requested Captain Squire to seize the types, than that the unhappy deluded public might no longer remain in the dark concerning the present contest, but that they should be furnished with a fair representation of facts, which I know never can happen whilst the press remains under the controul of its present dictators.   DUNMORE.'"[11]

The following three letters of Holt and the inventory of his estate are printed from the originals in the Manuscript Division of The New York Public Library:

HOLT TO SAMUEL ADAMS

New York 29th Jan'y 1776

Sir

Happening lately to be in Company of a Worker in Metals and speaking of the Cannon lately spiked up at King's Bridge; I asked him if he knew how

---
[11] *Penn. Gazette*, November 1, 1775, no. 2445, p. 1.

to clear the Cannon that Carleton had endeavoured to render useless by ramming them with Balls, at Montreal. He supposed that I had been applied to, to procure a Person who would undertake the Jobb, and last Night came to tell me he knew one who understood the Business & would do it on reasonable Terms; also that he understood repairing and putting old or damaged Muskets in Order, and would either buy them or make them fit for Service, and desired to know how much would be allowed on each piece of Cannon for clearing. I told him I had no Commission to do any thing in the Affair, but that as the Man he described, might be necessary to the Public Service, I would give Notice of him, and if it was thought proper to employ him, would let him know; In Consequence of which, I now give you this Intelligence. I could not know of my Informer, the Price expected on each Gun, but understood it would not exceed 20/ if the Number was considerable. The same Man also informed me of a Matter I had before heard of, and communicated to a Member of our Provincial Congress, viz. That the Emissaries of the British Ministry, particularly Governor Tryon, have for many Months past, been doing their utmost to engage all the Gunsmiths in America, in every Branch of the Business, to go for England, where they are promised high Wages and constant Employment for Life. That many of these in this Town, have actually enter'd into pay, & while they stay here are paid high Wages for not Working, nor instructing any Person in the Business; that a Number of these Workmen & many from this City, were sent home in the last packet, and every one who has any Skill in the Business here, has been tampered with — That even Convicts have been promised Pardons, 50 Guineas given for the Freedom of one in Maryland, & his Expences paid by Tryon to this City, from whence he was sent home. Two Convicts who lately were in Philadelphia, both Skilful Gunsmiths, enter'd into Contract with a Man here who fitted up a Shop for them, when they with some others, among whom were Servants went on board the Man of War, One of the Masters got Notice of it, sent his Principal Workman, (a Man in whom he confided, & who had a Wife here) to Governor Tryon, desireing his Assistance to get the Men back again. The Governor gave the Man a Letter to the Capt of the Man of War, who thereupon caused the Men all to leave the Ship, but before they reached the Shore, another Boat was sent after them, which carried them all on board the packet & they immediately sailed for England; the Man's Wife was sent after him by one of the last Ships. I believe you may depend upon the Truth of this Intelligence.

We still continue to be insulted by the two Ships of War close to our Docks, who not only seize all our Vessels that they can lay Hands on, and have put a stop to all our Navigation down the Sound between this & Hellgate, which is the nearest place to this City, that they now dare venture to, but on every Occasion Menace the Town with a Canonade. And if we do not improve the Time before the Spring, or the arrival of Troops and hips of War from England, I have not the least doubt but they will take possession of the Shores below and adjacent to Hell Gate, fill the Sound with their small Ships of War, & of Course stop all our Navigation in it, keep possession of long Island & make Excursions at pleasure upon the Mainland in New York, New Jersey, Connecticut & Rhode Island.

All this might be effectually prevented by our immediately erecting one or more strong Forts at & near Hell Gate and others on each Side below at the Narrows, with some Floats near them to obstruct the quick passing of Ships. Some floating Batteries would also be of the utmost importance. These Matters are absolutely necessary, & no Time ought to be lost. Whether or not our Provincial Congress are busied about other Affairs, so that they cannot attend to this, or that they expect Directions about it from the Continental Congress, I know not, but the Thing is not done, & the important golden Opportunity is hasting away — The Treasures of the Continent are in your Hands, all its Force under your Direction. If these Forts were only begun, with Vigour, in all probability the men of War would immediately decamp — if not should soon be able to secure them; I shall only add upon this Subject, now, that the Floats might be conveniently made in New Jersey, that I have seen a Scheme of the Form of them that I believe might be easily executed, and that Floating Batteries might be made either up the Sound, the North River, or in the Jersies.

I am not a little solicitous for the Completion of our important Design at Quebec, in which some of my most intimate Friends & near Connections are engaged and among their Inducements to it, had all that my Influence could give — particularly my worthy Friend Capt Lamb, and my Son in Law M^r ... azer Oswald, who tho' a Capt in the Expedition to Tyconderoga, Crown Point & taking the Vessels on the Lakes, went, thro' Friendship to Col^o Arnold & Zeal for the Service, with him a Volunteer, in his Expedition, without any Commission — The mortification I felt on hearing of our Repulse at Quebec, (tho' it cost some noble Blood, and caused a temporary Suspension of the Service of many valuable Men, by their Captivity, in which, I suppose, was included my Oswald, & Mr Lamb,) was abundantly compensated by hearing that they behaved bravely, becoming the Cause for which they fought, which, considering all Circumstances, I think the most important that was ever proposed to Mankind — *Freedom* and *Justice,* chased from every other Part of the Globe, also, where will they fly to, if driven from America? They must quit our wretched Globe and soar to Heaven. When I saw the Account of the gallant Behaviour of our Men, I was comforted for our Loss, when I saw the Names of my particular Friends among them, especially of my Boy Oswald, my mourning was turned into Joy, tho' he & they, as I suppose, are Prisoners. I was the more interested in the Conduct of this youth, because I had some Share in forming his political Principles. He came young from Falmouth, in England, where his Mother still lives, his Father, who sailed from that port Capt of a Ship, in the Jamaica Trade, has not been heard of for some Years. He served an Apprenticeship in this Town, where he behaved well & became connected with my Family. He was, like most Englishmen, prejudiced in Favour of the Ministerial Claims of Superiority and coercive Authority over the Americans, but was easily convinced of his Mistake, and ever since has been a hearty, zealous & active Friend to the great Cause in which we are now engaged. He is a very complete Master of the Military Exercise, which he learned from the Fagal Man[11a] of Col. Bernards Regiment, who was the most remarkably expert of any Man in the English Army. And I have been told there is no Man in our Army that is a better Master of the Manual Exercise than Mr Oswald. On the News of the Battle of Lexington, he was one of the Foremost Volunteers who set out from New Haven with Col. Arnold (of whom he has a high Opinion) to Boston, from whence they went on the Tyconderoga Expedition. In the Course of that Service, he went as a Courier, entrusted with the Care of the Business on which he went, two or more very long Journeys; in one of which, to the Continental Congress, he carried Col. Arnold's Proposals of an Expedition to Canada, on which he asked my Advice & Assistance. He was, in every Affair in which he was engaged, remarkably diligent assiduous & active. In one Day on this Journey he rode 95 and in another 115 Miles, and if every Advantage had been improved that was then in our Power, we should long since have been in quiet Possession of all Canada. I do not know by what Means the Canada Expedition was retarded, but it was retarded so long that it is almost Miraculous that it was attended with any Success at all. Col. Arnold it seems had been traduced, and had many Prejudices to encounter before he could receive his Commission, and then could not obtain such Offices for his Friends as were Necessary to induce them to follow him. Mr Oswald was very necessary to him, but he could obtain no Commission for him that was worth his Acceptance. However, personal Friendship for Col^o Arnold, and Zeal for the Cause, prompted Mr Oswald to go without any Commission, and with Joy I understand his Behaviour as a Soldier has done him Honour. The Wisdom and Dignity that has been conspicuous in all the Proceedings of the Continental Congress, leaves me no Room to doubt their favourable Notice of all who have distinguished themselves in the Public Service of America, especially in this Arduous Enterprise for the Reduction of Canada to join the general Interest. I have been thus particular, respecting Mr Oswald, that you may judge what Service he is most fit for, and that the Talents and Qualifications he posseses may be usefully employed in his Country's Service. He has Youth, Health, Hardiness, Activity, Courage & Perseverance. He is sober, diligent in Business & faithful to his Trust. He is skilful in the Manual Exercise, a very good Penman Accomptant & Arithmetician, with some Knowledge of Navigation, above all his Honour & Integrity may be safely relied on. If such a Person can be rendered useful to America, I doubt not the Continental Congress will cause his Talents to be properly applied, especially as the encouragement of those who have done well is a powerful Inducement to a laudable Emulation in others, to follow and improve upon the Example. Pray excuse my Prolixity. One Thing more I would mention.

The Post Office. Under the British Administration, the Primary End of it was, the augmentation of the Revenue, the public Conveniency, was but

---

[11a] So written for Fugelman.

a secondary Consideration. With us, at present, and I hope it will always be so, the Case is reversed; the public Conveniency, is the first Object. In comparison of this, the Revenue it produces, is hardly worth the least Notice, and in Order to give it all the Usefulness that might reasonably be expected from it, the Post Masters, from the highest to the Lowest should be indispensably enjoined to oblige all the Riders to carry and deliver at the proper places on their Respective Roads, all the Newspapers that should be brought to the post Offices for that purpose. In what I shall say upon this Subject, I am not in the least influenced by my own private Interest as the Printer of a Newspaper, but solely by a Regard to the publick good. I propose in a few Weeks, perhaps in one Week more, to discontinue the printing of a News paper, one great Reason of which Intention is, that I cannot get my Papers carried with any Regularity by the Posts, who consider the Carriage and Delivery of News papers, not as a matter of Duty, but Courtesy, and for this they are quite arbitrary in their Demands, as Caprice, or Avarice moves them, and often refuse to do the Business at all; many also sell or give away the papers they Carry, to any person that desires them. These Obstructions to the Regular Conveyance of News papers, is a very great Hindrance to their Circulation, and give infinite Vexation to those who send, and to those who ought to receive them, and greatly injure both in their Property, especially the Printer, who there by loses I suppose more than one half of the Country Customers he would otherwise have. But I mean now only to consider the Matter as it affects the Publick. As a mere Conveniency, the Carriage of News papers is of Importance to more than twenty Times as Many Persons as the Carriage of Letters is, and there are very few persons but who are much more solicitous to receive their News papers, than Letters, by the Post. But the great Use of News papers is that they form the best opportunities of Intelligence, that could be divised, of every publick Matter that concerns us, besides communicating many Useful Discoveries in Arts and Manufactories & many moral & religious Truths &c. It was by the means of News papers, that we receiv'd & spread the Notice of the tyrannical Designs formed against America, and kindled a Spirit that has been sufficient to repel them. But I need not to enumerate the advantages & Importance of a general Circulation of News papers, which I think are greater than of all the Letters carried by the Post — But it has been objected, that the Quantity of News papers is so great, as to overburden the Post Horses, and fill the Mail, so as not to have Room for or admit the Carriage of Letters & Dispatches — I answer that the mails should be enlarged or other Mails & Horses provided; and to defray the Expence, a reasonable, small allowance might be made, upon every Paper; by these means every one would get their Papers at an equal and easy Expence, which would give general Satisfaction, and remove every just Cause of Complaint. If two Horses were necessary, the smallest Boy, under the Care of a Man, might suffice for one of them, or the Horse might be led. The Experience I have had, both as the Printer of a News Paper, and as a Post Master, which I was for Many Years, convinces me that what I have now mentioned to you concerning News Papers, is just, and a Matter of very great Importance; The Government in England has been long verging towards Tyranny, the Increase of the Revenue, instead of increasing the National Strength & Happiness, has been applied to increase the Power and Influence of the Crown, which has at last almost swallowed up all the Rights & Liberty of the People. When an Imposition is granted upon any Article for Raising a Revenue for National Service, it is in Effect little different from giving so much to the King & his Ministers, to apply as they please. When a Tax was granted upon Letters, we may reasonably suppose it was intended News papers should be sent by the same Conveyance, since the Grant of a Tax was a Favour from the People to the Crown, for which they might have claimed the privilege of sending their News papers at an easy Expence. But we find the Ministry have instructed or permitted their Servants to discourage the sending of News papers by the Posts, either by a total Prohibition, or by exacting a high price for the Service, or at best granting it as a great Favour. It is the Continental Congress alone who can put this matter upon a proper Footing, it is not to be expected from a Post Master. Nor, in forming a Constitution ought any such power to be left in the Hands of a Single Person. Since a Post Office has been erected in Canada, I have heard several Complaints of the high postage, which the Soldiers & their Friends cannot well afford to pay — I believe it would be for the good of the Service if all Letters to and From Soldiers on Duty might go free of postage. I hope you will excuse this unconnected Epistle, being written in a Hurry at different Times, as I could get a Little Leasure. I am S^r

Your most obedi^t Servt

JOHN HOLT

[*Addressed:*] To

Samuel Adams Esqr

At

Philadelphia

HOLT TO NEW YORK ASSEMBLY

State of New York

Poughkeepsey 13th Feb^{ry} 1778

Gentlemen

Having after great Expence and Loss by the Enemy (at Danbury, on the Way) removed, with my Family, from New Haven to *Kingston,* on an Offer, by Letter, from a Committee of the Convention, to do the *Printing Business* of *this State,* in which I was engaged, at that Place, when, on Intelligence of the Enemy's Approach, the Assembly precipitantly broke up, having first in Order to transact publick Business, during their Recess, appointed a Council of Safety. These Gentlemen, offered and promised, in Case the Enemy should attempt landing at Kingston, to assist me with Waggons, not only for the Removal of the Printing Materials, part of which belonged to the State, but of my Family and private Effects. However several Circumstances concurring to render it improbable that the Enemy would attempt any Act of Hostility upon Kingston, or be able to hurt it if they should, the Inhabitants in general were unprepared for it, and when the Enemy landed, were destitute of the Means of Removal. Amongst the rest I shared the common Calamity — No Carriages were to be had, except four Waggons, when the Enemy were just at Hand, sent me by the President of the Council, which enabled me to remove about a Sixth part of my Effects, Viz One wearing apparel, three Beds, my Account Books, most of my Paper and the two best Fonts f printing Letter belonging to the State, which I preserved in preference to my own, the whole of which, together with my Press, all my printed Books, parchment &c. all my Household & Kitchen Furniture &c were totally destroyed or plundered by the Enemy, and my Family and Workmen obliged to take Refuge among the Neighbouring Inhabitants. In this Situation, on applying to the Council of Safety, I found it their Sense, that I should be supported as Printer to the State, that I should endeavour to keep my people together, & to collect materials for the commencement of Business again. To enable me to do this, they advanced me £200. amount Money of the State, which Sum, in several long Journeys, the purchase of sundry Necessaries, and my Removal to this place, has been long since all expended, together with some I have been obliged to borrow from a Friend. And yet, finding a considerable Deficiency of the sum requisite to the Recommencement of Business, and Subsistence of my Family, I am constrained to make this application to the Honourable Assembly of this State, requesting a further Supply of Money to enable me to do their Business, &c. I am

        Gentlemen

          Your most obedient hum^e se$_[$rv$^t_]$

            JOHN HOLT

P. S. I have since my arrival here, been long retarded from beginning Business, by the extreme Difficulty of procuring a few Necessaries — I am at last ready to begin composing, if the Assembly will please to furnish me with Copy of the Work first wanted. But I am still unable to do my Press Work, for Want of a Blanket, which I have, without Effect, used my utmost Endeavours to obtain.

[*Address missing*]

HOLT TO GERARD BANCKER

Poughkeepsie 23rd March 1783

Sir

I understand the Assembly have ordered me £200, to be paid by you out of the State Treasury. I have not seen the Order or Act so that I cannot tell the Tenor of it, only that it is for printing the Laws and Votes at this their last Meeting, which cannot go on without the Money, and are I suppose wanted with all possible Expedition. I shall therefore take it as a Favour if you will send an Order to the County Treasurer, who is my near Neighbour, if he has any money in his Hands, that he is to remit to you, that he will pay it to me, so far as to discharge the Order aforesaid or such part of it as the Balance amounts to — As soon as I see the Order, or Act, I shall acquaint you with the Contents of it, which you may also know, I suppose, by inquiring of Mr Lansing or any of the Albany Members and you'll much oblige

Your Friend & humᵉ Servᵗ

JOHN HOLT

[Address missing]

INVENTORY OF HOLT'S ESTATE

Inventory and Valuation of the Effects of Mr John Holt, late of the City of New York, Printer, deceased — taken at the Request and Solicitation of the Administratrix and Administrator to the said Estate. — New York, November 10. 1785 —

31 Setts of Laws of the State of N York..@ 55ˢ/	£85.. 5..—
6 Setts of Laws of the Sixth Session @ 2/9	16.. 6
1 Sett of Journals	1.. 5.. 2
59 Reams Waste Paper @ 4/	11..16..—
A Lot of old Books, consisting of old News-Books, — 20 Volumns (odd) — and a few old Magazines —	1.. 8..—
1 Old Pewter Ink-Stand	.. 3
Feathers of Two old Beds, & 1 dead feather bed	4..—..—
1 Corded Bedstead	.. 8..—
2 Bolsters and 3 Pillows (very old)	.. 6..—
1 Large & 1 small Iron Pot, Dish-Kettle & Grid-Iron	.. 8..—
1 Brass-Kettle & Pewter Tea Pot (very old)	..16..—
1 Pewter Tankard (old & battered)	.. 1.. 6
4 Old Trunks, and 1 Desk with sundry triffling Articles	1..—..—
1 Table, 1 Large & 1 small Tub	.. 6..—
2 Pails & 1 Case of Bottles	.. 7..—
3 Pair very old Snuffers	..—.. 6
3 Candlesticks (very old)	.. 1..—
Half dozen Knives & Forks (small size)	.. 3..—
4 Old Boxes	.. 1..—
1 Pair very old Hand Irons, and the Iron of another Pair —	.. 2..—
Carried Over —	£109..—..—

Amount brought forward	£109..—..—
2 Half Gallon Bottles 1*/. small Decanter & Tea Chest 2/6	..3..6
1 Sugar Box and a Trammel	..3..—
1 Pair Iron Tongs (old & burnt) & 3 Anchovie Bottles....	..1..6
7 old Homespun Sheets	1..—..—
20 Ounces & half of Plate, most of which has been in use near 40 Years....	9..12..1
1 Very old Cupboard & Leech Tub	..2..6
3 Pair Pillow Cases, Bread-Tray & saddle Bags	..6..6
4 Very old Blankets & 6 old pewter Plates	..16..—
1 Sute of old Curtains (for a single Bed)	1..10..—
Shelves & a broken Tea-Kettle	..3..—
Letter Case and a small Matrass	..8..—
Stone Pot and an old flute (broke)	..8..—
12 Bags, & 11 Horse Bags	1..—..—
Bread Basket & Bason	..2..—
Gun, Shot-Bag and Powder Horns (very old)	..16..—
Bed Quilt & Coverlets, and a Horse	4..12..—
1 Old silver Watch, Chain, &c & a family Seal	3..8..—
Slay-tackling & Saddle	1..16..—
Clothes and a wooden Bowl	10..—..—
2 Cork Screws	..1..—
Carried forward—	£145..9..1

Amount brought forward....	£145..9..1

Printing Materials, vizt

1 old printing Press	30..—..—
Iron of a Press (burnt at Esopus)	3..4..—
482 lb old Pica ....@ 10^d ℔ lb....	20..1..8
54½ lb 13 Line Pica ....@ 1/	2..14..6
102 lb 8 Line Pica ....@ 1/	5..2..—
39 lb Great Primer (Canon) ....@ 6^d	..19..6
103 lb Great Primer ....@ 1/	5..3..—
122 lb Pye of all Sorts............@ 4^d	2..—..8
157 lb Long Primer ....@ 1/	7..17..—
600 lb Originally bought, but now, after Near 2 Y^{rs} Use, supposed to be about 500 lb Burgeois....@ 1/9.......	43..15..—
5 Double & 3 single Frames (old)	1..17..—
15 Pair old Cases £6..— 7 Chases £2..16	8..16..—
3 Iron & 1 Wooden Composing Sticks	1..4..—
2 Royal Gallies 16/ 2 demy d° 8/—2 Quarto 6/	1..10..—
8 Sliding Gallies 8/. 1 Three Column d° 4/	..12..—
7 Letter Boards 3/. 1 Lye Trough 6/. 2 Buckets 1/	..10..—
	£280..15..5

We whose Names are hereunto subscribed, do certify & declare, that the forgoing Appraisement by us made, at the request of Mrs Elizabeth Holt and

Eleazer Oswald, is, in every Article & Thing in the same contained, appraised & valued according to the best of our Judgement.

          Anth'' Post

          John Wiley

          George Borkinbine

          Shepard Kollock

  City of New York ss: Be it Rembered [sic], that on the seven'th day of November one thousand seven hundred and eighty five John , Distiller, Anthony Post House Carpenter and George Borkinbine [s;] and on the day next following Shepard Kollock Printer all of the C'i of New York personally came and appeared before me Thomas Tredwell dge of the Court of Probates of the State of New York and being duly sworn on their Oaths severally declared that the Articles mentioned in the preceding writing signed by them the deponents are appraised and set down at their just and real value according to the best of their skill knowledge and information. —

          Thomas Tredwell

[*Endorsed*:] John Holt — Inventory of
       his Chattels —
       Recorded

Printed by Libri Plureos GmbH in Hamburg, Germany